GCSE in a week

Geog

Jon Marker,
Abbey Tutorial College
Series Editor: Kevin Byrne

Where to find the information you need

SUCCESS OR YOUR MONEY BACK

Letts' market leading series GCSE in a Week gives you everything you need for exam success. We're so confident that they're the best revision books you can buy that if you don't make the grade we will give you your money back!

HERE'S HOW IT WORKS

Register the Letts GCSE in a Week guide you buy by writing to us within 28 days of purchase with the following information:

- Name
- Address
- Postcode
- Subject of GCSE in a Week book bought
- Probable tier you will enter

Please include your till receipt

To make a **claim**, compare your results to the grades below. If any of your grades qualify for a refund, make a claim by writing to us within 28 days of getting your results, enclosing a copy of your original exam slip. If you do not register, you won't be able to make a claim after you receive your results.

CLAIM IF...

You're a Higher Tier student and get a D grade or below.
You're an Intermediate Tier student and get an E grade or below.
You're a Foundation Tier student and get an F grade or below.
You're a Scottish Standard grade student taking Credit and General level exams, and get a grade 4 or below.
This offer is not open to Scottish Standard Grade students sitting Foundation level exams.

Registration and claim address:
Letts Success or Your Money Back Offer, Letts Educational, Aldine Place, London W12 8AW

TERMS AND CONDITIONS

1. Applies to the Letts GCSE in a Week series only
2. Registration of purchases must be received by Letts Educational within 28 days of the purchase date
3. Registration must be accompanied by a valid till receipt
4. All money back claims must be received by Letts Educational within 28 days of receiving exam results
5. All claims must be accompanied by a letter stating the claim and a copy of the relevant exam results slip
6. Claims will be invalid if they do not match with the original registered subjects
7. Letts Educational reserves the right to seek confirmation of the Tier of entry of the claimant
8. Responsibility cannot be accepted for lost, delayed or damaged applications, or applications received outside of the stated registration / claim timescales
9. Proof of posting will not be accepted as proof of delivery
10. Offer only available to GCSE students studying within the UK
11. SUCCESS OR YOUR MONEY BACK is promoted by Letts Educational, Aldine Place, London W12 8AW
12. Registration indicates a complete acceptance of these rules
13. Illegible entries will be disqualified
14. In all matters, the decision of Letts Educational will be final and no correspondence will be entered into

Letts Educational
Aldine Place
London W12 8AW
Tel: 020 8740 2266
Fax: 020 8743 8451
e-mail: mail@lettsed.co.uk
website: http://www.letts-education.com

Every effort has been made to trace copyright holders and obtain their permission for the use of copyright material. The authors and publishers will gladly receive information enabling them to rectify any error or omission in subsequent editions.

First published 1998
Reprinted 1998, 1999 (twice)
New edition 2000

Text © Jon Marker 1998
Design and illustration © Letts Educational Ltd 1998

British Library Cataloguing in Publication Data
A CIP record for this book is available from the British Library.

ISBN 1 84085 3492

Design, artwork and production by Gregor Arthur at Starfish Design for Print, London
Editorial by Tanya Solomons

Printed in Italy

Letts Educational is the trading name of Letts Educational Ltd, a division of Granada Learning Ltd. Part of the Granada Media Group.

Plate tectonics

Test your knowledge

1 The earth's crust is split up into 7 large and many small .... plates. There are two types of crust, oceanic and continental.

2 Tectonic plates are moved by .... , in the mantle.

3 When plates move towards each other they can create a subduction zone. This can force magma to the surface creating a .... This is called a destructive plate boundary.

4 .... ridges are formed when plates move apart.

5 If two plates move side by side this is called a conservative margin. They can produce a build up of pressure causing an ....

6 When two plates meet they push together forming .... mountains to slowly rise.

7 People live in areas on the slopes of volcanoes because the .... is fertile.

8 People who live in more economically developed countries (MEDCs) are not as affected by volcanoes and earthquakes as people in less economically developed countries (LEDCs). This can be due to better warning systems and .... services.

✔ Turn to the next page to check your answers

Plate tectonics

Improve your knowledge

1 The earth's crust is split up into 7 large and many small **continental** or **tectonic plates**. There are two types of crust, oceanic and continental. Oceanic can be forced into the mantle, continental cannot.

2 Heat from the centre of the earth forces molten rock to rise in the mantle; this forms **convection currents**. Tectonic plates are moved by convection currents in the mantle.

3 When plates move towards each other they can create a subduction zone. Any oceanic crust will be forced into the mantle. The friction produced will melt rock, this can force magma to the surface creating a **volcano**. A deep sea trench will also be formed.

4 **Ocean ridges** are formed when plates move apart, exposing the mantle. Magma will rise and volcanoes will form along the boundary. These volcanoes are the mid-ocean ridge.

5 If two plates move side by side this is called a conservative margin. They can produce a build up of pressure causing an **earthquake**.

6 When two plates meet they push together, forcing the crust upwards and forming **fold** mountains.

7 People live in areas on the slopes of volcanoes because the **soil** is fertile. Volcanic rock breaks down to form fertile soils.

8 People who live in MEDCs are not as affected by volcanoes and earthquakes as people in LEDCs. This can be due to better warning systems and **emergency** services.

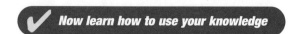
Now learn how to use your knowledge

Plate tectonics

20 minutes

EARTHQUAKE IN AWAJA ISLAND

On 17 January 1995, an earthquake measuring 7.2 on the Richter scale struck below Awaji Island across the bay from Kobe, a city and major commercial port in Japan. The quake caused buildings and bridges to collapse and fires to ignite throughout the city. In all, about 5,000 people died and more than 21,000 people were injured. More than 30,000 buildings were damaged by the quake and resulting fires. Population (1990) 1,477,410.

1 What effect did the earthquake in Kobe have on the local population?   **Hint ❶**

....

....

2 Suggest 2 reasons from the text why Kobe will take many years to recover from the earthquake.   **Hint ❷**

....

....

3 In 1993 16,000 people died in an earthquake in Latur in India, an LEDC. This earthquake was only 6.0 on the Richter scale. Explain why the Japanese government, a MEDC, was able to help people affected by the earthquake more than the Indian government.   **Hint ❸**

....

....

4 Why do people still live in areas of crustal instability? Hint **4**

....

5 What scale is used to measure earthquakes and earth tremors? Hint **5**

....

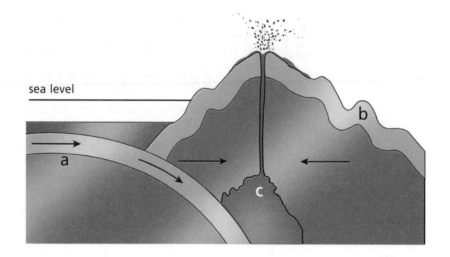

sea level

a

b

c

6 What type of plate boundary is shown in the diagram above? Hint **6**

....

7 What is causing the plates to move together? Hint **7**

....

8 Name the features a, b and c. Select from this list: fold mountain, volcano, subduction zone, oceanic crust, deep sea trench. Hint **8**

a ....   *b* ....

c ....

9 How is lava formed in the subduction zone? Hint **9**

....

✔ **Hints and answers follow**

Plate tectonics

1 Read the passage and highlight the things that would affect you or someone you know.

2 How long does it take to build a bridge or a building?

3 See *Improve your knowledge* section above.

4 See *Improve your knowledge* section above.

5 Answer in the text.

6 Is any new land being created? What is happening to the crust?

7 What is the crust on? Does anything move around the mantle?

8 See *Improve your knowledge* section above.

9 See *Improve your knowledge* section above.

Use your knowledge answers

1 Death and injuries; homelessness, destruction of property, businesses and loss of work; damage to infrastructure such as roads, water supply, fires; also psychological effects of earthquake and after shocks.

2 It will take many years to repair or replace the bridges and the 30,000 damaged buildings in the city.

3 LEDCs do not have the medical and emergency services of MEDCs. Poor quality housing will not withstand earthquakes; also there is less insurance.

4 Fertile soils which are good for agriculture, potential income from tourism, tribal homeland, pressure on land, scientific research, geothermal energy, lack of realisation of risk.

5 Richter scale measured on a seismograph, range from 0-9.

6 Destructive plate boundary.

7 Convection currents in the mantle. They are formed due to heat from the centre of the earth.

8 **a** oceanic crust.

   b fold mountain.

   c subduction zone.

9 Friction between the plates, as the oceanic plate is subducted under the continental plate, melts the rock.

Rocks and weathering

Test your knowledge

10 minutes

1. Igneous rocks are formed when .... from a volcano (e.g. basalt) or .... rising from the mantle cool and solidify (e.g. granite).

2. Sedimentary rocks are formed when eroded or weathered material is .... on the bottom of rivers or oceans. The material is compressed and cements together (e.g. limestone, sandstone).

3. Under intense heat and pressure all rocks can be structurally altered. These new rocks are called .... rocks (e.g. marble).

4. Physical weathering occurs when changes in the physical environment cause rocks to disintegrate. For example ...., water in cracks expands when it freezes, breaking lumps of rock off.

5. Chemical weathering decomposes rock slowly, altering its constituent minerals through chemical reactions. For example, ... oxygen reacts with minerals forming oxides which weakens the rock.

6. The breakdown of rocks by the action of plants and animals is called .... weathering.

✔ Turn to the next page to check your answers

Rocks and weathering

Improve your knowledge

10 minutes

1 Igneous rocks are formed when molten rock cools. This molten rock is found in two main forms.

- **Lava** from a volcano that cools on the surface forming extrusive igneous rocks (basalt).

- **Magma** which is found in the mantle rises closer to the surface and then cools slowly to form intrusive igneous rocks within the earth's crust (granite).

2 Sedimentary rocks are formed when eroded or weathered material is **deposited** on the bottom of rivers or oceans. Over time this material is buried causing the material to be compressed and to cement together (limestone, sandstone).

3 Under intense heat and pressure all rocks can be structurally altered. These new rocks are called **metamorphic** rocks. Limestone is metamorphosed to marble.

4 Physical weathering occurs when changes in the physical environment cause rocks to disintegrate. For example, **freeze thaw** – water in cracks expands when it freezes, breaking lumps of rock off. Freeze thaw can form scree slopes, which are large amounts of broken rock at the bottom of a mountain.

5 Chemical weathering decomposes rock slowly, altering its constituent minerals through chemical reactions. These chemical reactions reduce the bonding between the minerals. **Oxidation** – oxygen reacts with minerals forming oxides. This weakens the rock.

6 The other form of weathering is **biological** weathering. This breaks down rocks by the action of plants and animals.

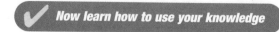

Now learn how to use your knowledge

Rocks and weathering

Use your knowledge

20 minutes

1 Fill in the boxes on the rock cycle. Choose from the following words: sedimentary, metamorphic, lava, magma, erosion, deposition, weathering, mantle.

Hint 1

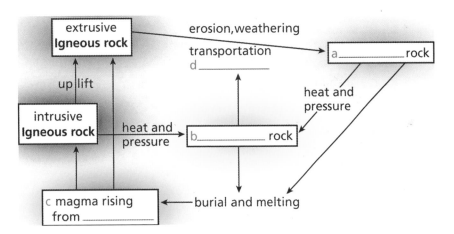

extrusive **Igneous rock**

erosion, weathering
transportation
d _____

a _____ rock

up lift

heat and pressure

intrusive **Igneous rock**

heat and pressure

b _____ rock

heat and pressure

c magma rising from _____

burial and melting

2 a What type of weathering is freeze thaw?

Hint 2

....

b Describe how this can break down rocks.

....

....

3 Hydration is the chemical reaction of water with a mineral within a rock.

Hint 3

a What type of weathering is this?

....

b How does it break down rocks?

....

4 Roots of plants often grow in cracks in rocks and over time may widen the crack. What type of weathering is this?

....

	Granite	Limestone
Landscape	Dartmoor – dominated by tors – rocky outcrops and heather moorland	Peak district – Karst landscape – limestone pavements and caves with grassland
How landscape is formed	Joints in the rocks, formed when the granite cooled, are widened by chemical weathering	Easily weathered by acidified water or rain
Uses	Aggregate and as polished stone	Used to produce cement and as lime in agriculture
Land use	Tourism and reservoirs	Tourism

5 How is granite formed?

....

....

6 What kind of weathering forms tors?

....

7 Reservoirs are man-made lakes, formed when rivers are dammed. Suggest two reason why upland areas are used for reservoirs.

....

....

8 List a positive and a negative effect that tourism could have on a granite and limestone upland.

....

....

✔ **Hints and answers follow**

Rocks and weathering

Hints

1 See *Improve your knowledge* section above.

2 a) and b)
Which type of weathering involves freezing and thawing of water?
See *Improve your knowledge* section above.

3 a) and b)
See *Improve your knowledge* section above.

4 Think about the nature of plants and what type of weathering this could be.
See *Improve your knowledge* section above.

5 See *Improve your knowledge* section above.

6 Answer in the table.

7 Is there a lot of rainfall on top of a mountain (see *Weather and climate* chapter)? Do many people use the land on top of mountains?

8 What effect would thousands of people have on the paths around these areas and the tor or karst landscape itself? Would people need somewhere to sleep or eat? See *Contrast in development and tourism* chapter.

Use your knowledge answers

1 a) Sedimentary b) Metamorphic c) Mantle d) Deposition.

2 a) Freeze thaw is physical weathering.

b) Water freezes in a crack or crevice of a rock. When this freezes it will expand pushing the rock apart. Over time this will weaken the rock, breaking bits off.

3 a) Chemical weathering.

b) Water reacts with a mineral within a rock. This alters the chemical constituents of the minerals in the rock, reducing the bonding of minerals within the rock and making it break down faster.

4 Biological weathering.

5 By the slow cooling of magma that has risen into the crust from the mantle.

6 Chemical weathering.

7 Large amounts of rainfall in upland areas. River valleys will create an ideal area to flood. Lack of any other land use. Lack of population to move before flooding.

8 Positive effects – Boost the local economy, by providing accommodation and food for tourists.

Negative effects – Large numbers of people will clamber over the area destroying the tor or karst landscape. Littering of the area. Footpaths will be eroded through over-use.

Rivers

Test your knowledge

1 Complete this diagram of the hydrological cycle.

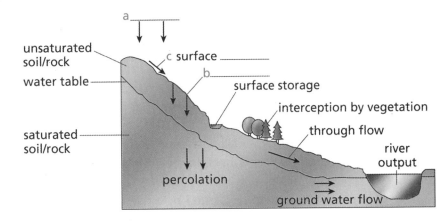

2 A .... is the area where water drains into a river. They are separated by higher land called watersheds.

3 The start of a river is called its .... and the end of the river is called an ....

4 Any silt, sand or stones carried by a river is called its load. This is .... when the water slows down.

5 Rivers wear down the surface of the earth by ....

6 A meander is a long bend found on the .... of a river. Meanders can develop into .... lakes.

7 People use water as a .... using rivers and lakes to further mankind's development.

 **Turn to the next page to check your answers**

Rivers

10 minutes

1   **a**   **Precipitation** – includes rain, snow, hail and fog.

      b   **Infiltration** – water that has soaked into the soil from the surface.

      c   **Surface runoff** – water that travels along the surface including streams and rivers.

2   A **drainage basin** is the area where water drains into a river. Any rain that falls into a drainage basin will flow into that river.

3   The start of a river is called its **source**. These are usually found in upland areas. The end of the river, where it meets the sea, is called an **estuary**.

4   Any silt, sand or stones carried by a river is called its load. This is **deposited** when the water slows down; on the banks (forming levees), where the river meets the sea (forming deltas or mud flats) or on the inside curves of a meander.

5   Rivers wear down the surface of the earth by **erosion** e.g. attrition.

6   A meander is a long bend found on the **floodplain** of a river. Meanders can develop into **ox-bow** lakes.

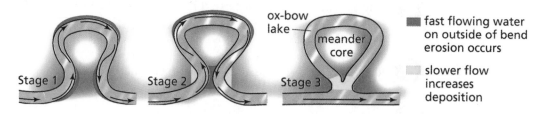

Stage 1   Stage 2   Stage 3

ox-bow lake

meander core

■ fast flowing water on outside of bend erosion occurs

▨ slower flow increases deposition

7   Water is considered a **resource** because of its many uses: drinking, washing, sewage removal, recreation, electric generation.

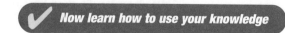

✔ *Now learn how to use your knowledge*

Use your knowledge

20 minutes

1 The diagram shows a cross section of a waterfall.

Hint ❶

Cross section of a waterfall

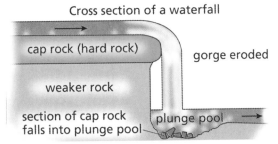

cap rock (hard rock)

gorge eroded

weaker rock

section of cap rock falls into plunge pool

plunge pool

a Suggest how erosion of the weaker rock has formed a waterfall.

....

b Why are large amounts of the cap rock found in the plunge pool?

....

2 a Suggest a reason why material is deposited on the banks of a river during a flood.

Hint ❷

....

b Levees are banks that have developed by deposition beside rivers. Why do humans increase the size of levees?

....

3 List three major human uses of a river?

Hint ❸

....

4 Draw a diagram showing how ox-bow lakes are formed, labelling areas of deposition and erosion.

Hint ❹

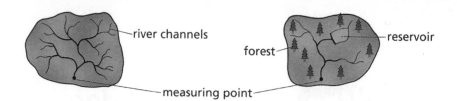

river channels

forest — reservoir

measuring point

Storm hydrograph for drainage basin A

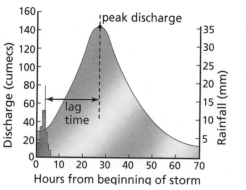

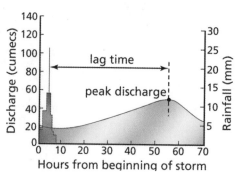

Study the storm hydrographs and the drainage basins shown.

5 Describe the difference in the discharges from the rivers.

Hint **5**

....

6 Suggest reasons for the difference in flow rate and lag time due to: a) the forest b) the reservoir.

Hint **6**

a ....

b ....

7 Is there any other factor that may affect the flow rate and lag time?

Hint **7**

....

8 Which drainage basin will flood more regularly? Give one reason for your answer.

Hint **8**

....

✓ **Hints and answers follow**

Rivers

Hints

1 a) Will weaker rock erode faster than hard rock?
How could this have formed the waterfall shown?

b) Will the hard rock never be eroded?

2 a) What happens to the velocity of the water when it leaves the channel of the river and floods?

b) Why would we want to have large banks by rivers?

3 See *Improve your knowledge* section above.

4 See *Improve your knowledge* section above.

5 Look at the graphs and write down what is happening on each. Are there any differences between the height of the graphs?

6 a) and b)
What effect would a forest or a reservoir have on the hydrological cycle and the amount of water reaching the measuring point?

7 Is there any other difference in the two drainage basins?

8 Floods occur when too much water is in the river. Which of the two rivers will have to move water downstream the fastest?

Use your knowledge answers

1 a) Waterfalls may form where the rock type forming the river bed changes from hard to soft rock (different geological properties). The soft rock is worn away faster than the hard rock leaving a hard cap rock. A waterfall occurs when the soft rock is worn away leaving a vertical drop.

   b) The softer rock will continue to erode, undercutting the cap rock which collapses to form boulders in the plunge pool.

2 a) When water leaves the river's channel in a flood, the velocity drops very quickly due to friction. Energy is lost and the river deposits material on the banks (levees).

   b) This will increase the amount of water that can be held in the channel of the river reducing the chances of flooding.

3 Recreation e.g. canoeing and fishing, drinking water, removal of sewage, production of electricity.

4 See *Improve your knowledge* section above.

5 Drainage basin A has a shorter lag time between peak rainfall and peak discharge and has a higher total discharge.

6 a) The forest area increases interception and therefore the amount of time surface runoff takes to get water to the channel.

   b) The dam has slowed down the total flow of the area.

7 Drainage basin B has fewer channels so water takes more time to get to a channel and more infiltration occurs.

8 Drainage basin A as the water discharges faster. This will increase the flow rate and increase the likelihood of flooding downstream.

Coastal landforms

Test your knowledge

10 minutes

1 Waves are caused by the movement of .... across the surface of the sea.

2 When waves meet the land they crash onto the shore, this is called the .... When they flow back towards the sea, this is called the ....

3 When waves hit land they can either .... material from the coast or they can .... material, such as sand, onto it.

4 Headlands are formed when weak rock is eroded leaving .... rock sticking out to sea. A beach is formed by deposited material.

5 Coastal areas have many uses. .... are tourist attractions. Estuaries make ideal sites for .... which stimulate industry in an area.

6 When waves crash onto the shore they can move material up the coast by the process of .... drift.

7 Coastal defences are used to stop the sea from .... the land.

Turn to the next page to check your answers

Improve your knowledge

10 minutes

1. Waves are caused by the movement of **wind** across the surface of the sea.

2. When waves meet the land they crash onto the shore, this is called the **swash** or **uprush**. When they flow back towards the sea, this is called the **backwash**.

3. When waves hit land they can either **erode** material from the coast or they can **deposit** material, such as sand, onto it.

4. Headlands are formed when weak rock is eroded leaving **resistant** rock sticking out to sea. The beach is formed by deposited material.

5. Coastal areas have many uses. **Beaches** are tourist attractions. Estuaries make ideal sites for **ports** which stimulate industry in an area.

6. When waves crash onto the shore, they can move material up the coast by the process of **longshore** drift. Waves move sand and pebbles onto the beach in the direction of the wave. Material rolls down the slope with the backwash. Material is thus moved along the coast in a series of zig-zags.

7. Coastal defences are used to stop the sea from **eroding** the land. Concrete blocks and boulders act as barriers to the waves stopping the land from being eroded. Groynes are wooden or concrete structures that jut out to sea and stop longshore drift.

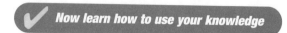

✔ *Now learn how to use your knowledge*

20 minutes

Use your knowledge

1 Study the diagram below showing the major stages of a headland being eroded to form a stump.

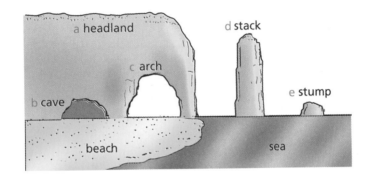

a How is a headland formed?

....

Hint **1a/b**

b Name a landform feature formed by deposition shown on the diagram.

....

Hint **1a/b**

c How is an arch formed from a cave?

....

Hint **1c**

d Why might you find bits of rock from the cliff on the beach?

....

Hint **1d**

2 a Which coastal areas are popular for tourists to visit?

....

Hint **2a/b**

b Which areas of a coastline will attract the most industry?

....

Hint 3

3 Humans have tried to stop the sea from eroding away the coastline. Use the diagram below to explain how a concrete wall or boulders could reduce erosion.

....

....

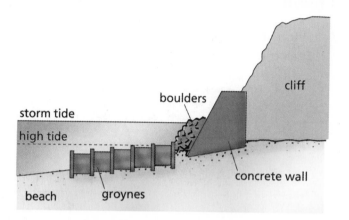

4 a What are groynes?

Hint 4

....

....

b How do they stop beaches being eroded by longshore drift?

....

....

5 a Which coastal areas are protected by coastal defences?

Hint 5

....

....

b Why is the whole of the UK not protected by coastal defences?

....

....

✔ **Hints and answers follow**

Coastal landforms

Hints

1 a) and b)
See *Improve your knowledge* section above.

    c) Think about the difference between an arch and a cave. What has happened?

    d) Where will most erosion occur on a cliff? Will this leave the cliff unstable?

2 a) and b)
See *Improve your knowledge* section above.

3 Where are the boulders and concrete? What erodes the cliff? What effect will the boulders and the concrete have on this erosion?

4 See *Improve your knowledge* section above.

5 Which areas have had large amounts of money invested in them for tourists or industry? Think about the cost of coastal defences and which sites on a coast will need protecting?

Use your knowledge answers

1 a) Headlands are formed when weak rock is eroded leaving resistant rock sticking out to sea.

   b) The beach.

   c) A cave is cut into a headland by erosion from waves. If a cave is eroded right through a headland this will leave an arch.

   d) Waves crash into the cliff and erode the bottom section creating a wave cut notch. The cliff above may collapse leaving material from the cliff on the beach.

2 a) Beaches are the most popular coastal areas for tourists to visit. Many people enjoy walking along cliffs.

   b) Areas where rivers meet the sea, forming estuaries, make the best sites for ports. Factories and industry will locate close to ports concentrating industrial activity around estuaries.

3 The concrete wall and boulders act as a physical barrier to the waves. This stops the cliff from being worn away, stopping erosion of the coast.

4 a) Groynes are wooden or concrete structures along beaches that jut out into the sea.

   b) The groynes will act as a barrier stopping material from moving along the beach. This reduces the movement of material by longshore drift.

5 a) Areas of importance: settlements, industrial areas and ports. Tourist resorts have groynes to conserve the beaches. Areas of geological interest are also protected.

   b) The cost of coastal defences stops them from being used around the whole coastline. Not all the coast needs protection.

Glaciers

23/7/09

Test your knowledge

10 minutes

1 Glaciers are large sheets or blocks of ice. ~~melt~~ most glaciers are found at the top of mountains.

2 Glacial areas are subject to weathering, mainly by ~~erosion~~ frost shattering .... , caused by the cold conditions.

3 Glaciers cause erosion when they move over the surface of the earth. Complete the table to see which types of erosion you know.

Name	Description of the action
a plucking	Rocks under a glacier freeze to the glacier and are pulled along when the glacier moves.
b	Any material caught under a glacier will grind the surface below like sandpaper.

4 Name the landforms shown in the diagram.

a Corrie

b ridge / arete

c Glacial peak

d pyramidal peak

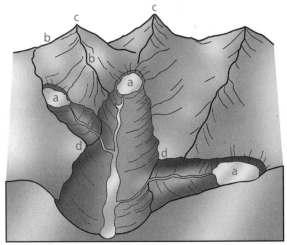

5 .... is made up of angular rocks which have been transported by a glacier and deposited when the temperature rises.

✔ Turn to the next page to check your answers

Glaciers

1 **Valley** glaciers are found at the top of mountains. They are formed in hollows where ice builds up before moving down the mountain side.

2 Glacial areas are subject to weathering, mainly by **frost shattering**, caused by the cold conditions. If water freezes in crevices (cracks in rock), it expands and forces the rock apart.

3

a) **Plucking**	Rocks under a glacier will freeze to its base. When the glacier moves down the mountain some of the rock is plucked from the surface and dragged along. This plucking can cause scratches called striations underneath the glacier.
b) **Abrasion**	Any material (little bits of rock) caught under a glacier will grind the surface below like sandpaper. The material is formed by freeze thaw action and plucking.

4 **a** **Corries** are deep rounded hollows with a steep back wall forming a rock basin. They are formed when plucking and abrasion wear down a hollow in the mountain under a glacier. After a glacier has melted the corrie may contain a lake or tarn.

b An **arête** is formed when two glaciers erode two corries back to back.

c A **pyramidal peak** is formed when three glaciers erode three corries.

d A **hanging valley** is formed when a small glacier meets a bigger glacier. The larger glacier erodes more material than the smaller glacier. This leaves a hanging valley above the valley floor.

5 **Moraine** is made up of angular rocks which have been transported by a glacier and deposited when the temperature rises causing the edge of the glacier to melt.

✔ **Now learn how to use your knowledge**

Glaciers

Use your knowledge

20 minutes

The diagram below shows a cross section through a valley glacier.

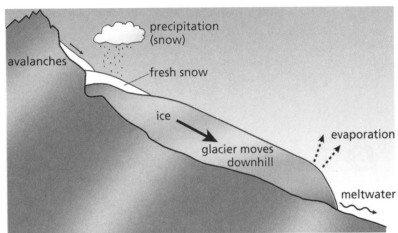

1 Use this diagram to explain how glaciers are formed.

Hint **1**

....

....

2 **a** What landform feature would you expect to develop in the hollow under the glacier?

Hint **2a**

....

b Outline the processes that cause this formation.

Hint **2b**

....

3 Why do corries fill with water?

Hint **3**

....

....

4 **a** What is moraine?

....

b Why are large amounts of moraine found after a glacier has
melted?

....

....

5 Why would a U-shaped valley left after glaciation make a good site for   *Hint* **5**
a reservoir or hydroelectric plant?

....

....

....

6 State four features which could characterise an area that has been   *Hint* **6**
under the influence of glaciers in the past.

....

....

7 Explain why rivers and glaciers form the following different landforms.   *Hint* **7**

River	Glacier
a) V-shaped valley	b) U-shaped valley
c) Waterfalls	d) Waterfalls

a ....

b ....

c ....

d ....

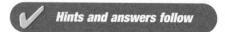

Hints and answers follow

Glaciers

Hints

1 Think about how ice formed from snow. See *Improve your knowledge* section above.

2 a) See *Improve your knowledge* section above.

b) How do glaciers form landforms? Is this deposition or erosion?

3 What do glaciers leave behind after they have melted?

4 a) and b)
See *Improve your knowledge* section above.

5 A reservoir is created by damming a valley. Why are glacial valleys better than the V-shaped river valleys? Hydroelectric plants produce electricity by holding back water behind a dam; how might U-shaped valleys make a good site for this?

6 What effect does a glacier have on the landscape of an area? Would you be able to identify these landforms after the glacier has melted?

7 To complete this section make sure you have worked through the unit on rivers.

Glaciers

Use your knowledge answers

1 In the zone of accumulation, snow falls in a hollow and is compressed to form ice as more snow falls on top. This is called the zone of accumulation. Gravity pulls ice downhill.

2 a) A corrie would be formed.

b) The glacier grinds out any hollows. Freeze thaw and plucking pull material from the sides creating a steep back wall.

3 Corries are natural basins and will collect rain or ice. Often large amounts of moraine have been left at the lip forming a dam.

4 a) Angular rock eroded and accumulated by a glacier.

b) Glaciers will have been eroding material for many years. This moraine will be deposited when the glacier melts.

5 A U-shaped valley will store a large volume of water behind a dam. They are usually in upland areas where there is little other land-use.

6 Any four of: moraine, corrie, pyramidal peak, arête, U-shaped valley, hanging valley, drumlin, roche moutonné, crag-and-tail, striations.

7 a) As rivers cut down into the valley floor, the valley sides are eroded and weathered.

b) Glaciers grind away obstacles like rocks by abrasion, widening and straightening the valley, forming a U-shaped trough.

c) Waterfalls are formed due to differential erosion of distinct rocks.

d) Large glaciers erode more material then smaller glaciers forming deeper valleys. When a small glacier feeds into a large glacier there is an abrupt change in valley height. Rivers flowing down these hanging valleys may form waterfalls.

Weather and climate

Test your knowledge

1 The term which describes the generalised weather conditions over 30 years is ....

2 When the sun heats up an area of land, the air above it rises. This creates areas of .... pressure. .... is the movement of air from areas of high pressure to low pressure.

3 As the air rises in the atmosphere, it cools. Any water vapour in the air will .... to form water droplets, which in turn form clouds and rain.

4 There are three different types of rain: convectional, ... , and frontal rain.

5 .... is the term used to describe rain, snow, sleet, mist and fog.

6 The sea heats up and cools .... than land. Any area of land close to the sea will have a .... climate, due to this heating and cooling effect.

7 When warm, moist air from the equator meets the cold drier air from the poles they do not mix. A .... is formed.

8 An .... is formed when air sinking over the UK creates a high pressure weather system.

✔ **Turn to the next page to check your answers**

 **Improve** *your knowledge*

10 minutes

1 The term which describes the generalised weather conditions over 30 years is **climate**, e.g. temperature and amount of rainfall.

2 When the sun heats up an area of land, the air above it rises. This creates areas of **low** pressure. **Wind** is the movement of air from areas of high pressure to low pressure.

3 As air rises in the atmosphere, it cools. Any water vapour in the air will **condense** to form water droplets, which in turn form clouds and rain, when the dew point is reached.

4 There are different types of rain: convectional, **relief** or **orographic** (formed over mountains), and frontal rain.

5 **Precipitation** is the term used to describe rain, snow, sleet, mist and fog.

6 The sea heats up and cools **slower** than land. Any area of land close to the sea will have a **maritime** climate, due to this heating and cooling effect. This means coastal areas have mild winters and mild summers.

7 When warm, moist air from the equator meets the cold drier air from the poles they do not mix. A **weather front** or **depression** is formed. The colder air mass pushes underneath the warm air giving large amounts of frontal rain or the warm air rises over the cold.

8 An **anticyclone** is formed when air sinking over the UK creates a high pressure weather system. (No clouds or rain, but fog at night.)

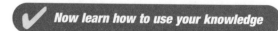
Now learn how to use your knowledge

Use your knowledge

1 **a** What is precipitation?

....

b Why is there more rain on top of a mountain?
Use the diagram above to help you find the answer.

....

....

c Name another form of rain other than relief rain.

....

2 What is the dew point?

....

3 **a** What is the climate of an area?

....

b Suggest two ways a maritime climate can be distinguished from a
continental climate, when the area involved is at the same latitude
on the earth's surface.

....

....

Hint **1**

Hint **2**

Hint **3**

4 The weather map shown describes the weather associated with a depression. **Hint 4**

Wind direction

↳ indicates a
ᵒ north-westerly
wind direction

Cloud symbols

○ clear sky
◔ sky covered
◑ sky covered
● sky covered
⊗ sky obscured

Fronts

▬●▬●▬ warm front
▬▲▬▲▬ cold front
▬●▬▲▬ occluded front

Wind speed

speed (knots)	force
○ calm	0
↳○ 3-7	2
↳○ 13-17	4

for each additional half feather, add 5 knots or an extra force

Pressure

Isobars drawn at intervals of 4 mb

Temperature

given in °C

Weather symbols

• rain
❜ drizzle

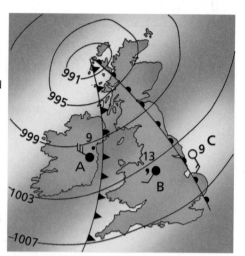

Describe any differences in temperature and precipitation in areas A, B and C.

....

5 What is the weather system shown on the map above called? **Hint 5**

....

6 Why do clouds form along the fronts? **Hint 6**

....

....

7 **a** What is an anticyclone? **Hint 7**

....

b Give three weather conditions that are associated with anticyclones.

....

Hints and answers follow

Hints

1 a) See *Improve your knowledge* section above.

   b) What happens to the wind when it meets a mountain?
     What is the temperature at the top of mountains?

   c) What are the other ways that air rises to form rain?

2 See *Improve your knowledge* section above.

3 a) What is the difference between climate and weather?
     See *Improve your knowledge* section above.

   b) What effect does the sea have on the climate of an area?
     Continental areas are a great distance from the sea.
     See *Improve your knowledge* section above.

4 Look at the weather map, list any differences you can see between the three areas.

5 See *Improve your knowledge* section above.

6 See *Improve your knowledge* section above.

7 a) and b) See *Improve your knowledge* section above.

Use your knowledge answers

1 a) Precipitation is rain, snow, sleet, mist and fog.

b) There is more rain on a mountain because when air is forced to rise over a mountain it cools causing any water vapour to condense to form clouds of water droplets. These will fall on top of the mountain as rain.

c) Either convectional or frontal rain.

2 The temperature (and altitude) when water vapour condenses to form water droplets.

3 a) The climate of an area is the general temperature, and amount of rainfall averaged over at least thirty years.

b) A maritime climate will be cooler in the summer, but warmer in the winter. The maritime climate will have rainfall all year round, whereas the continental climate will only have it in summer.

4 Area A   9°C, very windy, rain, full cloud cover.
Area B   13°C, windy, full cloud cover.
Area C   9°C, windy, no clouds.

5 A depression.

6 The air is forced to rise. This cools the air past the dew point, and water vapour will form water droplets and clouds.

7 a) A high pressure weather system.

b) Clear sunny sky, fog, mist, frosts, hot days, cold nights.

Agriculture

10 minutes

Test your knowledge

1 .... factors affect the type of animals or crops farmed in an area, such as climate and relief. Human factors also influence the type of agriculture through .... investment.

2 There are many types of farming carried out around the world. Fill in the table to show which types of farming you know.

Name	Description
....	The growing of crops, like wheat, barley, or rice.
Pastoral	Rearing of .... for food or to produce .... products.
Extensive	Using a large area for farming with few ....
....	A small area with large amounts of inputs to increase yield.

3 Farmers will use many methods to increase the amount of produce they can obtain:

a Fertiliser is used to increase the .... in the soil, stimulating plant growth.

b .... are used to kill insects or fungi which reduce plant growth.

c Extra water is added to dry areas to increase plant growth, called ....

d The removal of boundary .... will increase the size of fields.

4 Many farmers in LEDCs perform .... farming only, growing enough crops for their family to eat. In MEDCs farmers usually produce enough food to sell large amounts for profit, ... farming.

✔ **Turn to the next page to check your answers**

Agriculture

1 **Physical** factors affect the type of animals or crops farmed in an area, e.g. climate and relief. Human factors also influence the type of agriculture through **capital** investment.

2

Arable	The growing of crops, like wheat, barley, or rice.
Pastoral	Rearing of **animals** for food or to produce **dairy** products.
Extensive	Usually a large area is used for farming with few **inputs**.
Intensive	A smaller area is usually used, with large amounts of inputs to increase yield.

3 **a** Plants will use as many **nutrients** from the soil as possible. To make sure there is sufficient, farmers add more in the form of fertiliser.

b **Pesticides** are used to kill insects, fungi and weeds, and so help increase the yield from crops.

c Water is used for **irrigation** of crops when there is not enough rainfall.

d **Hedgerows** have been used for hundreds of years as boundaries to fields. If they are removed, the field size is increased as is the total farmable area.

4 Many farmers in LEDCs perform **subsistence** farming only, growing enough crops for their family to eat. In MEDCs farmers usually produce enough food to sell large amounts for profit, **commercial** farming.

✓ *Now learn how to use your knowledge*

Agriculture

20 minutes

Use your knowledge

Common Agricultural Policy (CAP)

The European Union, which includes the UK, has a Common Agricultural Policy (CAP). This aims to maintain a food supply for Europe. To achieve this, all agricultural markets have been stabilised maintaining a set price for the food farmers grow. This helps farmers plan for the future and ensures a fair standard of living. It is also aimed to give consumers reasonable prices for food, and to maintain jobs in rural areas.

There are problems with the CAP:

- Some farmers overproduce, creating a surplus which has to be sold off cheaply.
- Food production in Europe is more expensive than in USA or LEDCs, so Europe restricts the import of food from other countries.
- Farm sizes have increased to maximise machinery and profits. This has been at a cost to the wildlife that used to be found in hedges etc.
- Increased output also requires more fertilisers and pesticides.

1 Why did the EU form a Common Agricultural Policy?   Hint ❶

....

....

2 How did farmers gain from the CAP?   Hint ❷

....

....

3 What is the main type of farming found in the UK?   Hint ❸

....

4 Why has the CAP reduced the amount of wildlife in agricultural areas of the UK?   Hint ❹

....

....

5 What effect does the CAP have on international trade?

Hint **5**

....

....

6 *a* What is meant by the term increased output?

Hints **6a/**

....

b What methods can farmers use to increase output?

Hints **6a/**

....

....

c What method can be used to increase production in arid countries?

Hint **6c**

....

....

7 Are there any problems with the CAP?

Hint **7**

....

....

....

✔ *Hints and answers follow*

Agriculture

Hints

1 What use are farmers to large populated areas?

2 What changes has the CAP made to make life better for farmers?

3 Do farmers in the UK make a profit? What is this type of farming called?

4 How do farmers change the natural environment? Where does the wildlife in agricultural areas live and what are farmers doing to these areas?

5 International trade is the movement of products from country to country. See text for the answer.

6 a) and b)
See *Improve your knowledge* section above.

   c) What might limit the growth of plants in a dry place and how could you change this?

7 Look at the text again. Try to find problems with the CAP.

Agriculture

Use your knowledge answers

1 The aims of CAP are to stabilise agricultural markets, ensure Europe produces enough food for itself, maximise productivity and guarantee jobs in rural areas.

2 Farmers were guaranteed a set price for their products, enabling them to borrow money, buy machinery and implement modern farming techniques, knowing they could make repayments.

3 Intensive commercial farming: this can be arable or pastoral.

4 Farmers remove hedgerows and woods, and fill in ponds, to increase field size; this also removes the homes of most wildlife in agricultural areas. Excess nutrients cause eutrophication in rivers destroying the river wildlife. Increasing production can also increase soil erosion. Pesticides kill all insects, unwanted plants, and fungi, including rare species.

5 Farming in Europe is more expensive than in LEDCs and in the USA. To help European farmers compete, international trade is controlled. This reduces the development of LEDCs.

6 a) Increasing the amount of crops grown on the same area of land.

b) Increasing fertiliser will give plants plenty of nutrients, maximising growth. Pesticides will reduce competition for nutrients and light with weeds, and stop insects eating plants.

c) Irrigation will encourage crops to grow and raise yields.

7 The cost of the CAP is large, taking 70% of the EU budget. It creates excessive food supply, encourages the removal of hedgerows and drainage of wetlands, increases the use of fertilisers and pesticides and restricts international trade forcing up food prices.

Industry

 **Test** *your knowledge*

1 Fill in the table to test your knowledge of different types of industry.

Industry	Type	Examples
....	Raw materials	Farming, ... & ....
....		Manufacturing .... , ...
Tertiary	....	Teaching, distribution, transport
Quaternary	....	Research, microchip technology

2 Industry in LEDCs is mainly .... industry, whereas in MEDCs there is more secondary, tertiary and quaternary industry.

3 Fill in the blanks below listing all the physical and human or economic factors that affect the location of industry.

Physical factors

b_____	c site and land	
a raw materials		d_____ _____
Factory	
a_____		d_____
b markets	c_____ of scale	
e_____ policy		g_____ technology
f transportation	

Human or economic factors

4 Government policy can help to stimulate industry by giving .... or .... and by setting up industry friendly areas.

5 The majority of new factories are built on .... or industrial estates at the edge of towns.

6 .... industry has a free choice of site due to small amount of inputs that can be carried by lorries.

✓ *Turn to the next page to check your answers*

Industry

Improve your knowledge

10 minutes

1

Primary industry	Raw materials	Farming, **forestry** & **mining**
Secondary industry	Manufacturing	**Clothing, car-building** etc.
Tertiary industry	**Service** industry	Teaching, distribution, transport
Quaternary industry	**Information**	Research, microchip technology

2 Industry in LEDCs is mainly **primary** industry, whereas in MEDCs there is more secondary, tertiary and quaternary industry.

3 **Physical factors**

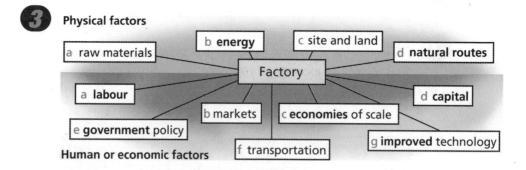

a raw materials
b **energy**
c site and land
d **natural routes**
Factory
a **labour**
d **capital**
b markets
c **economies** of scale
e **government** policy
g **improved** technology
f transportation

Human or economic factors

4 Government policy can help to stimulate industry by giving **grants** or **loans** and by setting up industry-friendly areas.

5 The majority of new factories are built on **business parks** or industrial estates at the edge of towns.

6 **Footloose** industry has a free choice of site, due to small amount of inputs that can be carried by lorries.

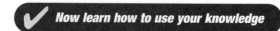
✔ **Now learn how to use your knowledge**

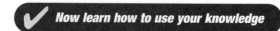

44

Industry

Use your knowledge

20 minutes

1 What is manufacturing industry?

....

....

Hint 1

2 Give two examples of primary industry.

....

....

Hint 2

3 Suggest two reasons why LEDCs have large amounts of primary industry.

....

....

....

Hint 3

4 What are the major types of industry you would expect to find in the UK?

....

....

....

Hint 4

5 How can governments affect the location of industry?

....

....

....

....

Hint 5

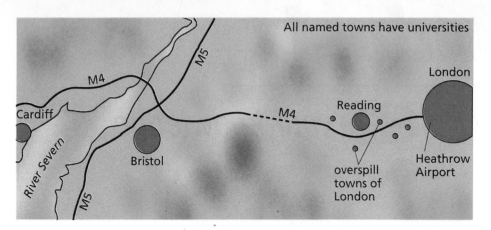

All named towns have universities

M4 · M5 · Cardiff · River Severn · M5 · Bristol · M4 · Reading · London · overspill towns of London · Heathrow Airport

6

Hint **6**

Study the sketch map above. Why would the area next to the M4 be a good area for footloose industry to locate?

....

....

7

Hint **7**

Where in Bristol would you expect to find new factories?

....

....

....

8

Hint **8**

List three benefits of new industry moving to industrial estates.

....

....

....

9

Hint **9**

Give two benefits to hi-tech industries of locating near to universities?

....

....

....

✔ **Hints and answers follow**

Industry

Hints

1 See *Improve your knowledge* section above.

2 See *Improve your knowledge* section above.

3 Do LEDCs have the expertise or investment to have any other industry? Do they have raw materials and a labour force?

4 Is the UK an MEDC? See *Improve your knowledge* section above.

5 What do governments decide that affects industry? Do governments try to increase the industry in any area specifically?

6 What does footloose industry need? Will it obtain that by locating next to the M4? Remember footloose industry still requires a labour force.

7 Where are the majority of new factories built? Is there any site that has very good transport links that might attract industry?

8 What does industry require? Are these provided by business parks or industrial estates?

9 Hi-tech industry uses the most up-to-date techniques to manufacture goods. This may include researching new techniques. Who is going to use this technology? Will they need to be highly skilled?

Industry

Use your knowledge answers

1 Manufacturing industry makes products from raw materials or several components.

2 Agriculture, forestry, fishing, mining of coal or minerals.

3 They have many farmers, large amounts of resources to exploit, e.g. forests and minerals, an abundance of cheap labour, and markets in MEDCs. They lack the money, technology, training and energy production needed for manufacturing.

4 The UK is an MEDC. There will be little primary industry and most farmers use machines. There will be some secondary industry, but large amounts of tertiary: e.g. lots of schools, distribution and transport, and a growing quaternary sector.

5 Governments build transport networks, control planning, give grants and loans, and can reduce tax burdens and administration costs.

6 Easy access to motorway and ports for transporting components and finished product. Good supply of workers and markets to sell products.

7 On the outskirts of the city, on an industrial estate with access to the M4 and M5.

8 They have good transport links, services such as electricity, water and drains, and space for car parking, storage or expansion.

9 Universities are sources of research facilities, highly skilled staff, and can train staff specifically for a company.

Test your knowledge

10 minutes

1 As countries become more developed they use more ....

2 The majority of energy in MEDCs comes from ....
.... , created by the plant and animal life that lived many years ago.

3 Fossil fuels release large amounts of .... when they are burned.

4 Many people in LEDCs still use .... for cooking and heating.

5 Hydroelectric power, wind, geothermal, tidal and bio-fuels, are all
.... sources of energy. They can be used many times over.

6 Many materials like metals or chemicals are obtained from their
.... , which are extracted from mines or quarries.

7 When these materials run out we must start to .... old products to
obtain new raw materials.

8 Large amounts of forest are lost each year to supply the demand for
.... and paper.

✔ **Turn to the next page to check your answers**

Improve your knowledge

10 minutes

1 As countries become more developed they use more **energy**, for industry, hospitals, education, transportation and leisure pursuits.

2 The majority of energy in MEDCs comes from **fossil fuels**, created by the plant and animal life that lived many years ago. Green plants grew by converting energy from the sun into chemical energy by the process of photosynthesis. Plant matter deposited underground was slowly converted into the **fossil fuels**, coal, oil, and gas. They are called non-renewable fuels because it would take millions of years to replenish deposits.

3 Fossil fuels release large amounts of **pollution** when they are burned. Carbon dioxide increases the greenhouse effect (see later). Sulphur and nitrogen oxides produce acid precipitation/rain.

4 Many people in LEDCs still use **fuelwood** for cooking and heating as there is little electricity or gas.

5 Hydroelectric power, wind, geothermal, tidal, and bio-fuels, are all **renewable** sources of energy as they can be used many times over.

6 Metals and chemicals are produced by processing their **ores**. These ores are dug out of the ground deposits either by mining or quarrying.

7 When the deposits of ores run out we will have to **recycle** old products, taking specific metals or chemicals out to create new raw materials.

8 **Timber** is still used in many processes: mainly to make paper and in the construction and furniture industries.

Now learn how to use your knowledge

20 minutes

Use your knowledge

The Greenhouse Effect

Energy from the sun is absorbed or reflected by the earth's surface. This is released into the atmosphere as heat energy. This heat energy is trapped in the atmosphere by greenhouse gases (GHG), e.g. CO_2, water vapour, methane.

The more GHG there are, the more heat will be trapped. This will lead to global warming or more precisely global climate change, as in some areas the climate may well be colder.

Any fossil fuels that are burnt increase the amount of CO_2 in the atmosphere.

1 Which energy sources release GHG?

Hint **1**

....

2 Which countries use the most energy?

Hint **2**

....

....

....

3 Which fuels do most countries use to generate electricity?

Hint **3**

....

....

4 **a** Give two examples of renewable energy sources. Hint 4

....

b Why do renewable energy sources not increase the greenhouse effect?

....

5 **a** How can we reduce the areas of forest cut down each year? Hint 5

....

....

b How can the planting of forests stop the build up of GHG?

....

....

6 Electricity produced by windmills does not produce any pollutants. It is available for use in many upland and coastal regions of the UK. Why is it not used more often in the UK? Hint 6

....

....

....

7 Why does the production of aluminium foil destroy large parts of the natural environment and create greenhouse gases? Hint 7

....

....

....

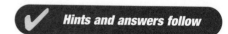
✔ **Hints and answers follow**

Energy and resources

Hints

1 Answer within text.

2 See *Improve your knowledge* section above.

3 See *Improve your knowledge* section above.

4 a) See *Improve your knowledge* section above.

b) Do they release any pollution when they are used?

5 a) What do we use the wood for and could we reuse or recycle this?

b) What do plants take up when they photosynthesise and how would this affect the GHG?

6 What do windmills look like? Would you like to live near to a hundred of them?

7 Think about the whole process of producing any industrial product from its raw material. Which parts use energy? Where do we get the raw materials from?

Use *your knowledge answers*

1 Fossil fuels, oil, gas or coal, release CO_2 when they are burned.

2 The industrialised MEDCs produce the most GHG. The industrial processes that MEDCs perform use large amounts of energy from fossil fuels.

3 Fossil fuels, oil, gas or coal.

4 a) Wind, tidal, wave, geothermal, biomass, hydroelectric, solar.

   b) They do not produce CO_2 or any other gas pollutants.

5 a) By recycling paper we could reduce the need to cut down forests.

   b) Trees, like all green plants, take up CO_2 from the atmosphere during photosynthesis. This reduces the amount of CO_2 to act as a GHG.

6 To many people, windmills are ugly to look at. Coastal and upland areas are most suited to generating wind power and these are also the most popular areas for tourism. Windmills also create a high pitched whining noise which carries for some distance and cannot, therefore, be located close to settlements.

7 Raw aluminium ore must be mined. Many of these deposits of ore are found under natural areas, like the tropical rain forest of Brazil. To remove the ore the area above the deposit will suffer some damage, and may even be totally destroyed. Large amounts of energy are used to transport ore: from mine to factory to be processed; from processing factory to the foil making factory, and finally to the markets and shops. All the energy used in the transportation and processing will give out GHG.

Population

Test your knowledge

1 .... refers to the spread of people in an area, whereas population density describes the number of people in an area usually in km^2.

2 .... factors influence the number of people that can live in an area; e.g. relief, climate.

3 A large population must also have ...., such as a good water supply, timber and minerals.

4 Human factors can also affect population size. .... policy will determine which areas receive more investment.

5 Parents in LEDCs need .... to help farm the land and ensure some children survive.

6 Parents in LEDCs may not use birth control methods because of .... beliefs.

7 Parents in MEDCs want small families, because they often desire material possessions and some women want ....

8 In LEDCs there are high death rates due to little .... and poor hygiene.

✓ Turn to the next page to check your answers

Population

Improve your knowledge

10 minutes

1 **Population distribution** refers to the spread of people in an area, whereas population density describes the number of people in an area usually in km².

2 **Physical** factors influence the number of people that can live in an area: e.g. relief, climate. Flat areas with good rainfall can support a large population whereas mountainous areas with lots of snow cannot.

3 A large population must also have **resources**, such as a good water supply, timber, minerals and food.

4 Human factors can also affect population size, as **government** policy will determine which areas receive more investment. This can affect the road or rail lines to an area and how much employment is available.

5 Parents in LEDCs need **large families** to help farm the land and ensure some children survive. Many children in LEDCs die in their infancy.

6 Parents in LEDCs may not use birth control methods because of **religious** beliefs.

7 Parents in MEDCs want small families, because they often desire material possessions and some women want **careers**. They use contraception and this has lowered the birth rate.

8 In LEDCs there are high death rates due to little **medical care** and poor hygiene. This can be due to lack of money. Over-grazing or poor weather can destroy crops and lead to famine which can kill many people in LEDCs.

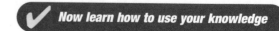

Now learn how to use your knowledge

Population

Use your knowledge

1 Why does the death rate fall in a country?   Hint ❶

....

....

2 How can the education of women reduce the birth rate?   Hint ❷

....

....

3 Why is the population of MEDCs declining?   Hint ❸

....

....

4 How can governments reduce the growth in a population?   Hint ❹

....

....

5 **The Demographic Transition Model (DTM)**   Hint ❺
This model has been based on the changes in population growth that
have occurred over the last 500 years in European MEDCs, and is now
used to compare LEDCs today.

Stage 1	Stage 2	Stage 3	Stage 4
BR and DR are high.	BR high DR falling.	BR falls DR falling slower.	BR and DR fluctuate depending on factors such as epidemics, disasters, and trends in each generation.

BR = birth rate, DR = death rate

57

The term life expectancy means the age people are expected to live to.

a How does average life expectancy of a population change from stage 1 to stage 4 of the DTM?

....

b What are the major causes of death in stage 4 of the DTM?

....

....

6 What problems will an increasing population have for an LEDC?   **Hint 6**

....

....

....

7 List two physical factors that: **Hint 7**

a can support a large population:

....

....

b cannot support a large population:

....

....

8 How can government policy affect the overall population of a region?   **Hint 8**

....

....

....

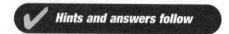
Hints and answers follow

Population

Hints

1 Why do people live longer as countries develop?

2 What will women want to do once they are educated? Will they know the problems associated with having a large family?

3 Why do people not want to have children? Are there any benefits to not having children?

4 What information or help could governments give to reduce the birth rate?

5 a) How long will people live in stage 1 and stage 4?

   b) Look at the text again.

6 Think about the cost to government of raising an individual from a child to a working adult.

7 See *Improve your knowledge* section.

8 See *Improve your knowledge* section.

Population

Use your knowledge answers

1 Improved health services, better hygiene and improvements to water and sewage works reduce incidence of disease. Better agricultural techniques improve food production and diet.

2 Educated women have more choices. They understand that having many children in rapid succession is bad for their body and reduces their life expectancy. They may choose to work instead.

3 Pensions are given by the government to help the old. People want material possessions such as cars or holidays. Women may want careers. Couples put off having children until they are older.

4 Governments can provide free contraceptives and give women information about family planning. Reductions in infant mortality encourage people to conceive fewer children.

5 a) Life expectancy increases.

b) Old age. Epidemics and disasters causes fluctuations in stage 4.

6 Increasing populations need to be fed, housed and educated. LEDCs cannot provide these basic services. Spending on welfare reduces the investment available to industry.

7 a) Flat areas, good rainfall, fertile soil, pleasant climate.

b) Mountainous areas, low or heavy rainfall, extremes of climate.

8 Governments determine where investments are made in a country, and where roads and railways are built. Increased investment leads to increases in population size.

Settlements

Test your knowledge

1 The .... of a settlement relates to the relief or soils of the land it is built on. The .... describes where the settlement is in relation to other settlements or rivers.

2 Settlements develop in different areas due to the .... factors of that area, e.g. near a river or spring for water supply, or near flat land to provide a food supply.

3 Settlements have a distinct shape or .... , e.g. linear or nucleated.

4 To make life efficient, settlements provide certain .... for the local population.

5 Settlements have developed to provide different .... This could be a mining, tourist or dormitory settlement.

6 Towns grow to meet the demand for new homes, and the opening of new factories and new shops. This development is called ....
....

7 .... are areas designated to stop towns merging and provide areas of recreation for the local population.

8 The distance people are willing to travel to a settlement depends on the settlement's .... of ....

9 Each type or size of shop or service requires a .... population if it is to survive for many years.

✔ *Turn to the next page to check your answers*

Settlements

Improve your knowledge

10 minutes

1 The **site** of a settlement is the area of land which it is built on, in terms of relief, soils or water supply. The **situation** describes the settlement in relation to other settlements, rivers and communication routes.

2 Settlements develop in different areas due to the **physical** factors of that area, for example near a river or spring for water supply.

3 The **form** of a settlement is dependent on its physical and human features.

linear settlement

road

nucleated settlement around crossroads

4 To make life efficient, settlements provide certain **services** for the local population, e.g. welfare, retail, transport and entertainment.

5 Settlements have developed to provide different **functions**, e.g. market towns, tourist resorts.

6 Towns grow to meet the demand for new homes, new factories and new shops. Most new growth is called **urban sprawl** or urbanisation.

7 **Green belts** are areas designated to stop towns merging and provide areas of recreation for the local population.

8 Major settlements provide services or entertainment for people living within their **zone of influence**.

9 Each type of shop requires a certain number of people to support it. This is called its **threshold** population (e.g. 200 people for a post office, 50,000 for a supermarket).

Now learn how to use your knowledge

Settlements

Use your knowledge

20 minutes

Conurbation	City	Town	Village	Hamlet

← Population increasing

1 Which type of settlement has the smallest population?

Hint 1

....

2 What is a zone of influence?

Hint 2

....

....

3 Which type of settlement would you expect to have the largest zone of influence?

Hint 3

....

4 What is the relationship between the population size of a settlement and the number of services in a settlement?

Hint 4

....

....

5 What are green belts?

Hint 5

....

....

6 Where would you expect to find a green belt area?

Hint 6

....

....

7 Why is there pressure to build on green belt land?

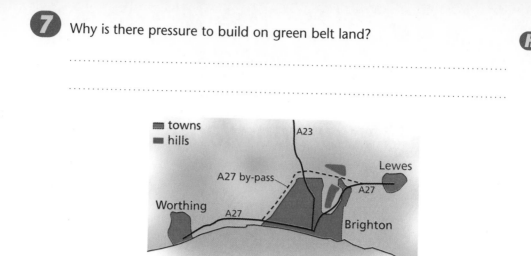

Hint **7**

8 How have the physical and human features of Sussex affected the growth of Brighton?

Hint **8**

9 How have the routes A27 and A23 shaped the development of Brighton?

Hint **9**

10 There are many small local service centres spread around Brighton.

Hint **10**

a What is a local service centre?

b Why has the centre of Brighton got a wider range of shops and goods than a local service centre?

✓ *Hints and answers follow*

Settlements

Hints

1 The list of settlements given is in order of population size.

2 Why do people from other areas travel great distances to visit large cities?

3 Which type of settlement will have the most services to attract people?

4 Do more people need more services?

5 See *Improve your knowledge* section above.

6 See *Improve your knowledge* section above.

7 Where is it easiest to build factories, on the site of old derelict factories or on open fields?

8 Look at the map of Brighton. Where has growth occurred? What physical features surround Brighton?

9 Look at the map of Brighton. How have the roads affected the development of the urban area?

10 a) What services do you need on a daily or weekly basis? These are provided by a local service centre.

b) Do more or fewer people go to the city centre? Does that affect the amount of shops that can be supported?

Settlements

Use your knowledge answers

1 A hamlet.

2 The distance people are willing to travel for the services.

3 Conurbations.

4 The larger the population of a settlement the greater the number of services it can maintain. Large settlements will exceed the threshold population for the shops and services.

5 They are areas where no development or building can occur.

6 They are found around the outside of larger settlements.

7 There is a lack of space in the centre of towns to build new homes and industry. It is cheaper and easier to build on the outskirts of towns and these are more desirable locations for housing and industrial development.

8 Brighton started to grow along the sea front, and has slowly expanded inland. Being on the coast it has developed a semi-circular shape compared with the more usual circular shape of other towns. There are two chalk hills in Brighton which have not been developed.

9 The town has developed more along the routes of the two roads.

10 a) Local service centres often include a doctor, dentist, small supermarket, post office, newsagent, bus stops, public houses. They serve a single residential community.

b) More people will use the town centre than any one local service area. This increases the threshold population, increasing the number of shops that can be supported, and the range of goods available.

Urbanisation

Test your knowledge

10 minutes

1 Urbanisation is the movement of people from .... areas to urban areas.

2 .... are urban areas that have joined together to form one settlement.

3 The centre of an urban area is called the .... This area has the tallest buildings.

4 In MEDCs people have started to move out of the city back to the country. This is called .... People leave the city due to poor living standards, for example, cramped conditions, ... and ....

5 People in LEDCs leave rural areas due to poor quality of life, starvation or ....

6 Many people in LEDCs move to urban areas to find .... or for a higher standard of living.

7 Urban areas in LEDCs have many people who cannot afford houses so they live in poor quality huts in ....

8 Many people migrate from rural areas to work in cities every day; this is called ....

Turn to the next page to check your answers

67

Urbanisation

Improve your knowledge

1 Over the past 200 years many people have moved from **rural** areas to urban areas in the UK, a process known as urbanisation.

2 **Conurbations** are urban areas that have joined together to form one settlement.

3 The central area of urban areas has become the **Central Business District**. It has tall buildings because the price of land is expensive.

4 In MEDCs people have started to move out of the city back to the country. This is called **counter-urbanisation**. People leave the city due to poor living standards, e.g. cramped conditions, **pollution** and **crime**. Pollution from traffic and industry affects health.

5 People in LEDCs leave rural areas due to poor quality of life, starvation or **overpopulation**.

6 Many people in LEDCs move to urban areas to find **jobs** or for a higher standard of living.

7 Urban areas in LEDCs have many people who cannot afford houses so they live in poor quality huts in **shanty towns**.

8 Many people migrate from rural areas to work in cities every day, which is called **commuting**.

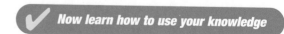

✔ *Now learn how to use your knowledge*

Urbanisation

20 minutes

Use your knowledge

Study the following table showing the change in size of major cities around the world. All figures are in millions.

1970	1985	2000 (estimate)
New York 16.5	Tokyo 23	Mexico City 28.5
Tokyo 16	Mexico City 18.7	Sao Paulo 25
London 10.5	New York 18.2	Tokyo 20.3
Shanghai 10	Sao Paulo 16.8	Shanghai 18.7
Mexico City 8.6	Shanghai 13.3	New York 17.5
Sao Paulo 7.1	London 7.9	London 6.9

1 Which cities are in MEDCs?   *Hint 1*

....

2 Which 2 cities have grown the most?   *Hint 2*

....

3 Why has the population of London decreased over the last 20 years?   *Hint 3*

....

....

4 Many people work in London but live in other towns.   *Hint 4*
What is this called?

....

5 What could be done to improve the standard of living in the urban   *Hint 5*
areas of MEDCs?

....

Shanty towns

Shanty towns are poor quality housing areas, mainly small wooden shacks that have developed around factories or alongside roads. They have no water pipes or drains to remove sewage, which can give rise to the spread of diseases, such as cholera and typhoid. Education and employment is limited and there is no public transport. These poor conditions are stressful for families and teenagers may drift into a life of crime.

To improve the life of the people who live in shanty towns, governments have started self-help schemes whereby people are given materials to build their own settlements and are lent money at low interest rates to set up community projects.

6 Explain why people in an LEDC may wish to leave rural areas.

Hint **6**

....

....

....

7 Why would they want to move to urban areas?

Hint **7**

....

....

8 Why are shanty towns common in LEDCs?

Hint **8**

....

....

9 Suggest reasons why people in shanty towns die young.

Hint **9**

....

....

10 What can be done to help people in shanty towns improve their standard of living?

Hint **10**

....

....

✔ *Hints and answers follow*

Urbanisation

Hints

1 Japan, the UK and USA are MEDCs; which cities are associated with these countries?

2 Work out the answer from the table.

3 See *Improve your knowledge* section above. Why are people leaving cities in MEDCs?

4 See *Improve your knowledge* section above.

5 What are the problems of living in cities in MEDCs? See *Improve your knowledge* section above. How can we solve these problems?

6 See *Improve your knowledge* section above. Why are people leaving rural areas?

7 See *Improve your knowledge* section above. Why are people attracted to cities?

8 LEDCs have growing populations of people in rural areas. Where are they likely to move to find jobs? Will an urban area have homes for all these people?

9 Answer is within the text and *Improve your knowledge* section.

10 Answer is within the text.

Urbanisation

Use your knowledge answers

1 New York, Tokyo, and London.

2 Mexico City and Sao Paulo have doubled in size.

3 Many people dislike the pollution, crime, lack of space. They have moved to a more rural environment (counter-urbanisation).

4 Commuting.

5 Reduce the number of cars and scale of industry in a city to reduce pollution. Increase open space by removing some buildings and creating parks. Increase the amount of employment which may reduce crime.

6 Increased pressure on land; overpopulation; starvation; mechanisation has reduced number of jobs on land; poor quality of life due to lack of services and entertainment.

7 To find jobs, better quality housing, an education or medical treatment, a reliable source of food, or better religious and social amenities.

8 People are dissatisfied with poor quality of life in rural areas and have false expectations of life in cities. They migrate to cities which are already crowded and cannot cope with the influx of new residents.

9 Poor water supply and lack of sewage works increase the spread of diseases. Lack of medical care; high birth rate, due to lack of education and contraception; high infant mortality.

10 Self-help schemes are now common. Community projects are supported financially. Building materials are provided.

Contrast in development and tourism

Test your knowledge

1 The .... is the amount of money earned by a country divided by its population.

2 There are many barriers to stop a country developing, such as a large, growing .... or lack of capital.

3 Development within a country will also vary. This can be seen in the .... model. Many workers will .... from areas that are less developed into the developed area, i.e. from peripheral areas to the core area.

4 Many LEDCs used to be run by or were .... of European countries.

5 Tourists from MEDCs visit LEDCs because the .... is usually hot and a different culture is experienced.

6 Tourists bring .... into the economy of an LEDC.

7 Tourists require .... and infrastructure of a higher standard than the local people.

8 Tourists will require people to serve them, so local people will have to speak many ....

9 Farmland may be sold or taken from local people and used for .... instead of farming.

✔ **Turn to the next page to check your answers**

Contrast in development and tourism

Improve your knowledge

1 Indicators are used to assess the level of development within a country. For example, the **Gross National Product** or GNP is the amount of money earned by a country divided by its population.

2 A large growing **population** or lack of capital can stop a country developing. A large population must be fed and educated.

3 Development within a country will also vary. This can be seen in the **core periphery** model. Many workers will **migrate** from areas that are less developed or from peripheral areas, into the developed or core area.

4 Many LEDCs used to be run by or were **colonies** of European countries.

5 Tourists from MEDCs visit LEDCs because the **weather** or **climate** is often hot, a different culture is experienced and costs are low.

6 Tourists bring **capital** or **money** into the economy of an LEDC. Tourists spend money on food, accommodation and local products.

7 Tourists require more **services** and infrastructure of a higher standard than the local people e.g. medical centres and roads.

8 Tourists will require people to serve them; so local people will have to speak many **languages**. Local people may not be as educated as people from the major cities, and will not get the best work in the tourist industry.

9 Farmland may be sold or taken from local people and used for **tourism** instead of farming.

 **Now learn how to use your knowledge**

Contrast in development and tourism

20 minutes

Use your knowledge

	Number of children per woman	% of people without clean water	Mortality per 1,000 of under fives
Uganda	7	61	190
Algeria	5	88	133
Bangladesh	5	45	61
UK	2	0	9
Spain	1	1	9

1 *a* What does the number of children per woman indicate about the development of a country?

Hint ①a

....

....

b Suggest two reasons for the large number of children who die before the age of five in Uganda.

Hint ①b

....

....

2 *a* Using the information in the table only, name a country which is economically developed.

Hint ②

....

b Give one reason for your answer.

Hint ②

....

3 *a* A large growing population will slow development. Why is this an internal barrier to development of an LEDC?

Hint ③

....

....

Tourism in Kenya

Kenya, an LEDC, is on the equator in Africa. Kenya is renowned for the wildlife found in the Masai Mara National Park. Many people from MEDCs go on safari to see lions, elephants and zebra. They either camp or stay in hotels and are transported around in vans to see the animals.

The local people are the Masai, a nomadic tribe. They used to live beside the wildlife grazing their cattle. Now they are restricted to grazing their animals in set areas outside the national parks. This has forced the Masai to earn a living by performing traditional dances for tourists, instead of cattle farming.

Kenya also has beautiful beaches and coral reefs.

4 What effect will tourism have on the local tribes in the Masai Mara?

Hint **4**

....

....

5 What advantages are there to Kenya of having tourists visit their country?

Hint **5**

....

....

6 Why are the beaches in Kenya more attractive to tourists than those in UK?

Hint **6**

....

....

✔ Hints and answers follow

Contrast in development and tourism

Hints

1 a) The number of children is another measure of birth rate. How does birth rate vary with development?

   b) Is Uganda very developed? Does it have a large number of doctors and would this affect child mortality?

2 Use the indicators to work out which is the more developed. Explain how the different indicators enabled you to select some countries and reject others.

3 See *Improve your knowledge* section above.

4 Use the information in the text.

5 What do tourists bring into a country and what do they take home?

6 Where is Kenya and what is the climate like? Do they have cold winters?

Use your knowledge answers

1 a) The more developed a country the lower the birth rate.

b) Poor water supply will increase the likelihood of children contracting diseases that may kill. There is little health care in less developed countries like Uganda. There may not be a regular food supply in Uganda due to lack of money in agriculture.

2 a) Either Spain or UK.

b) Spain has the lowest population growth rate. UK has 0% of population without clean water.

3 A large population will increase the amount of money that a government will have to spend on education and medical health. This will reduce the amount of money available for investment in industry and infrastructure, reducing development.

4 Tourism attracts migratory workers. Tourists and new workers require accommodation which takes up land. It changes the way the local people live e.g. they are only allowed to graze a restricted number of cattle to protect the wildlife.

5 Tourists will bring capital into the country, boosting the economy of Kenya and enabling them to improve their infrastructure. Tourism will also stimulate education as local people decide to learn foreign languages. This will all help Kenya to develop.

6 Kenya is on the equator and therefore experiences hot weather all year round. This means tourists are likely to enjoy sunshine and high temperatures. The UK is in mid-latitudes. Even in the summer the temperature is lower in the UK.

Trade and Aid

Test your knowledge

1 Trade between countries is needed to provide all the .... (food, energy, raw materials) any country requires.

2 If a country imports/buys from other countries more than it exports/sells to other countries it has a ....

3 LEDCs have mainly got primary industry and thus export .... for MEDCs' manufacturing industry. LEDCs need manufactured goods like computers which are .... from MEDCs.

4 To increase the amount of trade, countries group together to form trade treaties. This removes the import duties or .... from trade.

5 The UK is joined to other countries in Europe by a trade agreement; they form the ....

6 Aid is the giving of .... such as food, money or technology from MEDCs to LEDCs.

7 .... aid, e.g. food, clothing, medicine or shelter is given when a disaster, such as volcanic eruption or famine affects an LEDC, whereas long term aid aims to help a country develop.

8 Aid is designed to improve the .... of .... for the people who live in LEDCs.

✓ Turn to the next page to check your answers

Trade and Aid

Improve your knowledge

10 minutes

1 Not every country has all the different **resources** that they require. These can be raw materials or manufactured goods.

2 If a country imports more than it exports it will have a **trade deficit**. It will have to borrow money to pay for these goods and have less money to spend on development.

3 LEDCs have mainly got primary industry and thus export **raw materials** for MEDCs' manufacturing industry. LEDCs need manufactured goods like computers which are **imported** from MEDCs.

4 Trade treaties remove **tariffs** which are put onto products when they are imported making it more expensive to buy foreign products. By removing these tariffs, more people are stimulated to buy foreign goods.

5 The UK is joined to other countries in Europe by a trade agreement; they form the **European Union**.

6 Aid is the giving of **resources** such as food, money or technology from MEDCs to LEDCs.

7 **Short term** aid, e.g. food, clothing, medicine or shelter is given when a disaster, such as a volcanic eruption or famine, affects an LEDC. Long term aid aims to help a country to develop, providing help with water supplies or farming.

8 **Quality of life** is generally considered to be the amount of services any person in a country has available to them.

Now learn how to use your knowledge

Trade and Aid

Use your knowledge

20 minutes

The diagram shows the areas UK trades with

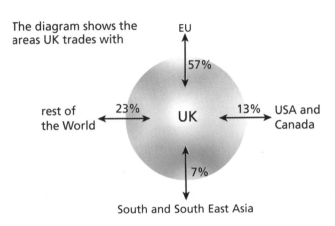

EU

57%

rest of the World ←→ 23% UK 13% ←→ USA and Canada

7%

South and South East Asia

UK total exports
£190.5 billion

UK total imports
£221.7 billion

1 What are imports?

Hint **1**

....

2 **a** What have the EU countries signed?

Hint **2a**

....

b What effect has this had on the amount of trade the UK has with the EU?

Hint **2b**

....

....

3 What is a trade deficit? Does the UK have one?

Hint **3**

....

4 **a** What is a tariff?

Hint **4a**

....

b Why does the UK impose tariffs on imported goods?

Hint **4b**

....

An Aid programme in Kenya

Actionaid is an English charity that works around the world. It has been working in Kenya since 1974, trying to eradicate poverty. Three schemes they have initiated are:

- Helping 53,000 people in the area of Kyuso gain access to clean, safe water.
- Establishing savings and credit groups so that farmers can buy ploughs and oxen for agriculture.
- Providing services such as immunisation, family planning and treatment for diarrhoea in the slum district of Nairobi.

5 **a** How has Actionaid helped the farmers of Kenya to improve their agricultural output?

Hint 5a

....

....

b Suggest why this is using appropriate technology.

Hint 5b

....

....

6 How does aid from charities differ from direct aid from government?

Hint 6

....

....

7 How does short term aid help an LEDC in crisis?

Hint 7

....

....

8 How will increasing the amount of clean water available increase life expectancy in Kenya?

Hint 8

....

....

✔ *Hints and answers follow*

Trade and Aid

Hints

1 See *Improve your knowledge* section above.

2 a) What did the UK sign with other countries in Europe? See *Improve your knowledge* section above.

b) Answer is in the diagram and in *Improve your knowledge* section above.

3 See *Improve your knowledge* section above and diagram.

4 a) What do countries put on the price of an imported product?

b) What does this do to the price of imported products compared with those manufactured in the UK?

5 a) Answer is within the text.

b) Appropriate technology involves using techniques that can be used after the aid programme has finished.

6 How do charities get their money and is this a constant supply? Where do governments get their money?

7 See *Improve your knowledge* section above.

8 See *Population* chapter. Will a clean water supply increase or decrease the spread of disease in a country? How will this affect the life expectancy of the population of the country?

83

Trade and Aid

Use your knowledge answers

1 Imports are resources or goods brought from another country.

2
  a) The EU countries have signed a free trade agreement.

  b) This has increased the amount of trade within the nations who have signed the agreement. 57% of all our exports are sold in the EU.

3 A trade deficit occurs when a country imports more goods than it exports. The UK has a trade deficit.

4
  a) A tariff is a tax placed on imported goods when they are sold within a country.

  b) This makes them more expensive than home-produced goods encouraging people to buy goods made in their own country, creating jobs within the country.

5
  a) They have helped them buy ploughs and oxen to grow more crops.

  b) Oxen and ploughs are in common use throughout Kenya; the aid programme is making them available to more people. The benefits will continue even when the aid stops.

6 Aid from charities comes from donations by individuals in MEDCs and is regulated by the timing of donations. Money from governments is guaranteed more regularly.

7 It provides food, medicine and shelter. The donor country may even send doctors and nurses to help the affected LEDC.

8 Diseases like cholera or typhoid thrive in dirty water supplies. Clean water reduces the number of deaths from these diseases, thus increasing life expectancy in Kenya.

1 Read the extract below and answer the following questions.

The Montserrat Crisis – 4 July 1997

After 400 years of lying dormant, Chances Peak volcano, on the island of Montserrat, has been slowly pumping out ash and lava for the past 16 months. On the 27 of June this year Chances Peak covered most of the island with ash and mud. The capital, Plymouth, was covered in mud and many buildings and roads were destroyed. During the eruption 23 people were killed and many were injured.

Many islanders have fled to Antigua and other islands in the Caribbean: some have come to the UK as Montserrat is a former colony of the UK. The south of the island is still a danger area so the remaining population is now concentrated in the north in emergency shelters.

Montserrat's natural beauty and climate attracted many tourists. Many wealthy people from the USA and Europe came to enjoy the beautiful hills and beaches of this Caribbean island.

Help for the island

A group of pop stars, including Sir Paul McCartney, Sir Elton John and Eric Clapton, performed a concert at the Royal Albert Hall. All money from the concert is to go to help the islanders of Montserrat. The British government sent HMS Liverpool to the area. The crew have built emergency kitchens and showers.

a) How did the volcano affect the people of Montserrat?

b) What is a subduction zone?

c) Use the diagram to explain why the volcano erupted.

d) Explain why people continued to live on Montserrat after the volcano started to erupt.

e) What type of aid is being given to the people of Montserrat by the UK government?

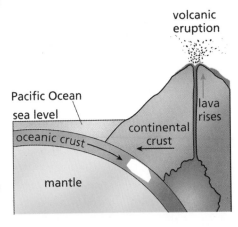

f) How will the building of kitchens and showers help the islanders?

g) What was a colony?

h) Why was this island good for tourism?

i) Suggest two benefits and two disadvantages of tourism for the local people.

j) Why has the eruption affected many businesses around the world, not just local people?

2 a) Annotate the diagram to explain how an ox-bow lake develops.

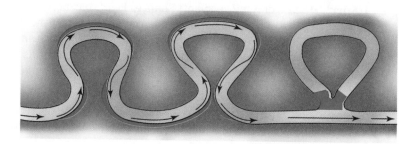

b) Suggest two reasons why an urban area may build concrete banks beside a river.

c) Rain falling within an urban area will be collected in storm drains which lead to the nearest river. What effect does this have on the flow of a river?

3 a) What are groynes?

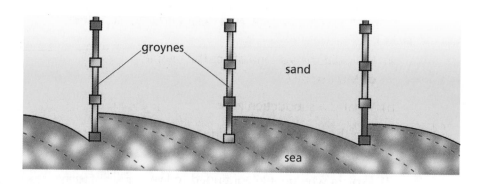

c) Why does the area in the diagram have coastal defences?

4 a) How was the pyramidal peak formed?

b) Are there any other signs of glaciation?

c) What type of physical weathering may be found when an area is under a glacier?

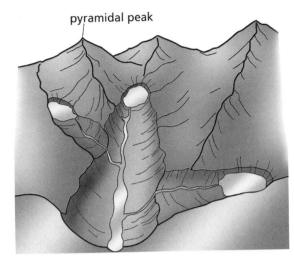

pyramidal peak

5 a) What is the weather feature shown?

b) How does it affect the weather over the UK?

c) Why is there more rain on top of a hill?

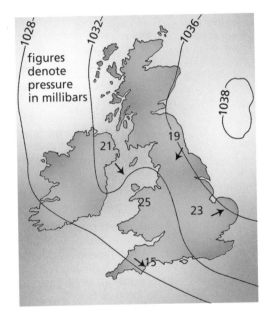

figures denote pressure in millibars

6 a) Why do farmers use fertilisers?

b) Suggest a reason why farmers in the UK and France use more fertilisers than Bangladesh and Pakistan.

c) Explain why farmers in Pakistan might use irrigation to increase their crop growth.

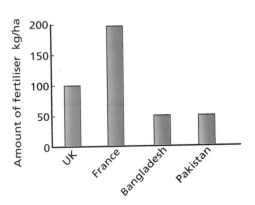

7   Production of steel in Wales

Initially the iron industry was found within the valleys of the Brecon Beacons (see map). The iron industry was replaced by steelworks in the 1860s.

The production of steel involves the use of a blast or electric arc furnace, a large oven heated by coal or electricity. The blast furnace is used to melt iron ore and many of the impurities are removed by the addition of limestone. This molten metal can be mixed with oxygen to remove carbon producing steel.

When the iron ore and coal deposits ran out the steel industry moved to Port Talbot, a deep water port on the Welsh coast (see map).

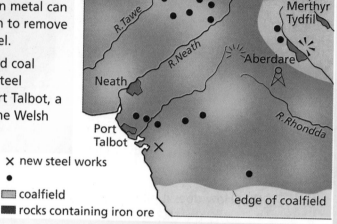

key

ℳ coalmine   ✕ new steel works

꙳ limestone quarry   ▢ coalfield   •

꙳ iron ore quarry   ▰ rocks containing iron ore

a)   Why did the iron and steel industry develop in the areas shown?

b)   Why did the steel industry move to the area shown?

c)   What type of industry is:
   - i)   coal mining?
   - ii)   steel production?

d)   What type of rock is limestone?

e)   Name an economic use of limestone.

f)   Many people visit upland areas to see the limestone landscape. How does this affect the economy of the area?

8

a)   Petroleum is produced from oil. What type of energy source is oil?

b)   Which type of country uses the most petroleum?

c)   Name two pollutants that are produced when fossil fuels are burned.

9

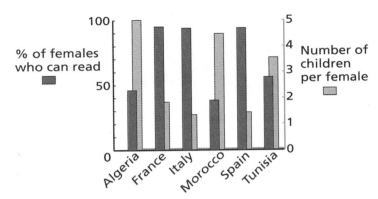

% of females who can read ■

Number of children per female ▨

a) Describe the relationship between female literacy and the number of children a woman conceives.

b) Suggest a reason for this relationship.

c) Give two reasons why people in Africa may not use contraception.

d) Suggest two reasons why the population of Italy, an MEDC, is falling.

10

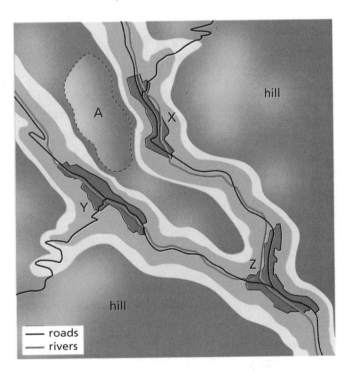

a) Use evidence from the map to suggest why area A is sparsely populated

b) List three reasons why the three settlements X, Y and Z were located in these areas.

c) How have the roads affected the growth of settlement Z?

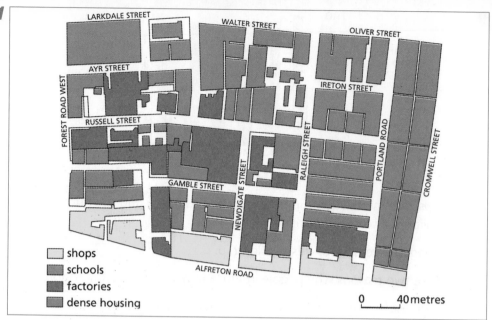

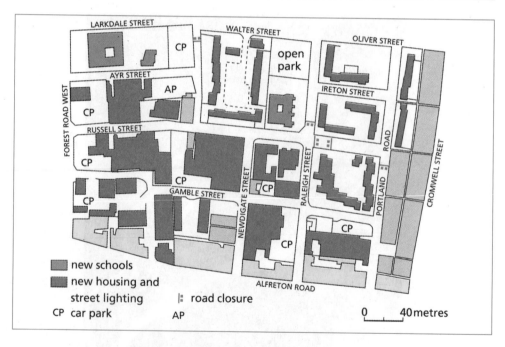

A city area has been redeveloped.

a) How have town planners improved the area in the diagram for the local residents?

b) What is counter-urbanisation?

c) How might the changes shown stop counter-urbanisation from occurring?

Answers

1 a) 23 people were killed, buildings were destroyed, many people have left the island or moved to emergency shelters. The tourism industry has stopped so opportunities for economic growth and employment are greatly reduced.

b) An area where one continental plate moves under or subducts another plate.

c) The oceanic plate moved under the continental plate causing friction. This melted some of the plate which, being less dense, was forced to the surface to form a volcano.

d) This was their birthplace or where they had lived for many years. Their jobs and friends would be on the island. The climate and area are beautiful.

e) Short term aid.

f) The kitchens will provide food for the local people, reducing the impact of the disaster. Showers will enable people to cleanse themselves of the dust and mud from the volcano.

g) A colony was an area conquered and then run by a European country.

h) Good climate, warm and sunny. Beautiful hills and beaches. The relaxed atmosphere of the Caribbean people.

i) Benefits: Improved services for the local people, e.g. doctors and transport. Large number of jobs, e.g. cleaning and serving the tourists in hotels.

Disadvantages: Land prices will rise as land is bought for tourist complexes reducing the traditional farming lifestyle. Increase in people migrating into the area looking for employment. May have an increase in crime.

j) Hotels are expensive to build and run: most are owned by rich individuals or multi-national companies who are not necessarily based on Montserrat.

2 a)

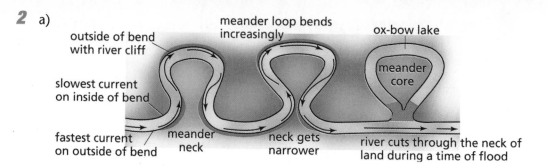

outside of bend with river cliff

meander loop bends increasingly

ox-bow lake

meander core

slowest current on inside of bend

fastest current on outside of bend

meander neck

neck gets narrower

river cuts through the neck of land during a time of flood

b) To stop the channel from eroding the bank or moving left or right. To increase the amount of water held by the channel to reduce incidence of flooding.

c) Storm drains reduce the amount of time it takes water to enter the river by surface runoff, therefore the flow of the river will increase rapidly. This may lead to flooding downstream of the urban area.

3 a) Groynes are wooden or concrete structures constructed on beaches to reduce the movement of material by longshore drift.

b) The swash of the waves hits the beach at an angle moving material with it. The backwash of the wave rolls straight down the beach. Material therefore moves along the beach in a series of zig-zags. (Movement is to the right in this diagram.) This is called longshore drift. Groynes act as physical barriers to drift and deposited material accumulates behind them.

c) Many tourists visit the area to sit on the beach. The coastal defences, by stopping the beach from moving to the right, are protecting the local economy.

4 a) Three glaciers have eroded the mountain producing three steep sides at the top of the mountain.

b) Corries, arêtes, hanging valleys, U-shaped valleys.

c) Frost shattering.

5 a) An anticyclone.

b) A clear sky, no clouds, sunny days. Cold nights with some dew, fog or mist in the morning.

c) Wind is forced to rise over mountains. As it rises in the atmosphere it cools and any water vapour will turn to water droplets at the dew point, forming clouds and rain.

6 a) Fertilisers increase the nutrients available to a crop in a field. This will increase the crop growth of the field, making more profit for the farmer.

   b) The UK and France are MEDCs, therefore the farmers have more money to buy fertilisers. The technology is available to produce and apply fertilisers and there are more places to buy fertilisers. The UK and France may need to use more fertilisers as fields may become exhausted due to over production.

   c) Pakistan has a hot climate and lack of water may be limiting the growth of crops. Irrigation will increase the water in the fields and therefore the growth of the crops.

7 a) There was an abundance of raw materials for the iron and steel industry. There were people to work in the factory and land was available for building the factory.

   b) When local supplies were exhausted raw materials had to be imported by ship. To reduce transportation costs the steel industry moved to the port.

   c) i)   Primary.
       ii) Secondary.

   d) Sedimentary.

   e) Uses: to produce cement, as road aggregate, as a building material, as lime in agriculture, in the steel industry, and as a tourist attraction.

   f) The economy of the area will expand, due to people wanting to stay in hotels, eat at restaurants and buy gifts. This will increase employment in the area but may reduce work in traditional jobs/crafts.

8 a) A non-renewable, fossil fuel.

   b) MEDC or Developed.

   c) Carbon dioxide (a greenhouse gas), sulphur and nitrogen oxides (producing acid rain).

9 a) As more women learn to read they have fewer babies.

   b) Educated women want careers. They realise that having many children reduces their life expectancy. They may have read newspapers containing information about population control in their country. They may know about family planning techniques.

c) Contraception may not be available or affordable in their area. They may not know about it. They need or desire a large family to work the land. Infant mortality may be high. Religious or cultural reasons.

d) Women want careers. Infant mortality is low. Families don't need to have many children. The parents may want material possessions or more holidays. High costs of child care are a disincentive.

10 a) Area A is an upland region with few flat areas for settlement.

b) There was flat land, a water supply, communication routes (a road) and an area for agriculture.

c) The settlement has grown along the sides of the road.

11 a) Road closures stop traffic using the residential areas as short cuts. Increased open areas for children and adults. Reduced population density. Increased car parking. Reduction of industry in urban areas. Improved lighting.

b) People who lived in urban areas moving to rural areas.

c) Reduction in traffic and industry reduces pollution in the area. More open spaces reduces cramped conditions. Improved lighting reduces crime or fear of crime.

Books are to be returned on or before
the last date below.

LIBREX-